T0358072

1

© Knowledge Books and Software

This is a necklace worn by the
First People.

© Knowledge Books and Software

© Knowledge Books and Software

This is a shell necklace.

© Knowledge Books and Software

5

© Knowledge Books and Software

The First People wore kangaroo necklaces.

© Knowledge Books and Software

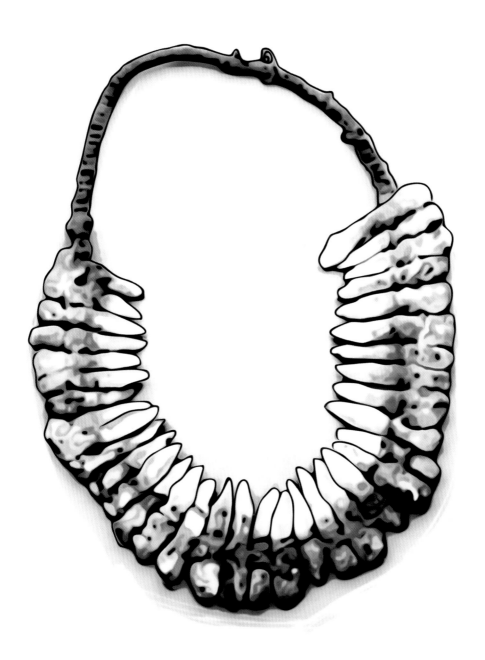

7

© Knowledge Books and Software

Some wore string ties.

© Knowledge Books and Software

© Knowledge Books and Software

Ornaments were used for dancing.

10

© Knowledge Books and Software

11

© Knowledge Books and Software

Hats were also worn for ceremonies.

© Knowledge Books and Software

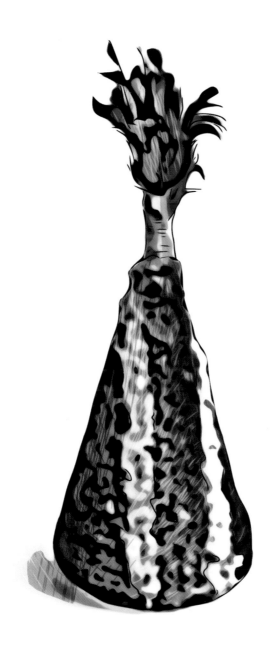

13

© Knowledge Books and Software

The people wore feathers for dancing.

© Knowledge Books and Software

15

© Knowledge Books and Software

Ears were decorated for dancing.

© Knowledge Books and Software

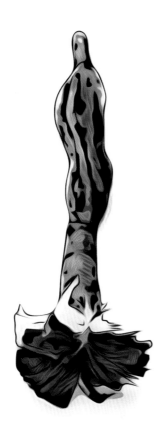
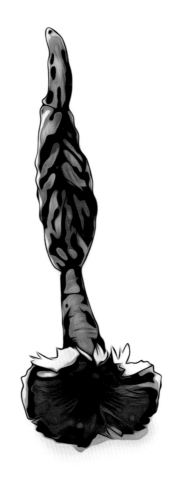

17

© Knowledge Books and Software

Shells were worn as necklaces.

© Knowledge Books and Software

© Knowledge Books and Software

This kangaroo tooth necklace was worn as decoration.

© Knowledge Books and Software

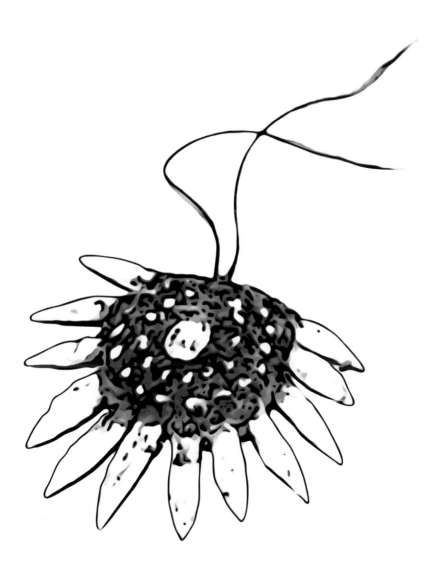

21

© Knowledge Books and Software

This dancing headwear is from Torres Strait.

© Knowledge Books and Software

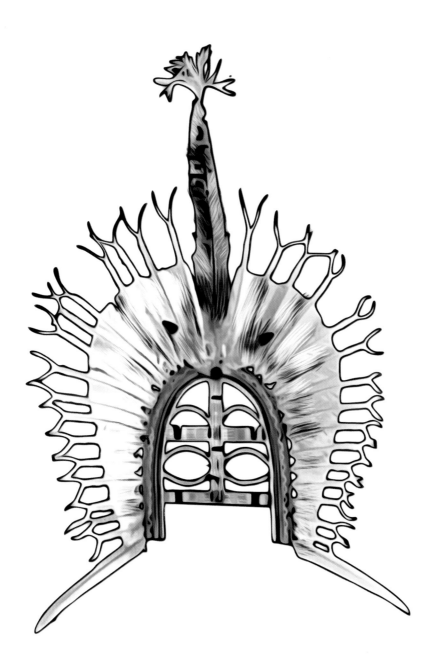

23

© Knowledge Books and Software

Word bank

ceremonies

ornaments

necklace

worn

shell

kangaroo

string

feathers

dancing

people

decorated

decoration

headwear

Torres Strait

sister

© Knowledge Books and Software